Creatures, Critters, Beasts and Varmints

(A Poetic Guide to Ozark Wildlife)

By Ken Slesarik

DEDICATION

To Kenny, Cathy and Bonnie, you are the reasons why I write and I love you dearly.

CONTENTS

ACKNOWLEDGMENTS

A standing ovation to my friend "The Chuckster," without your support and cover art this project would not have been possible. Thank you to the students and staff of Esperanza Music Academy, poetry rocks and so do you! A special thank you to David Harrison, Janet Wong and Sylvia Vardell, I have learned much from observing you. Thank you Veronica for your unconditional love and a final thank you to my family for your encouragement and belief in my message.

Call me Bob
(A poem for two voices)

You keep denying you're a Lynx, dear cousin, that just really stinks.	**Lynx**
We're as different as chalk and cheese so call me Bob if you please.	**Bobcat**
You "doth protest too much, methinks." You're in the family of the Lynx.	**Lynx**
That's Shakespeare, if I'm not mistaken, with a good voice to beg bacon.	**Bobcat**
You always had that tendency, to joke but it can't get to me.	**Lynx**
Having fun, well that's my job. Don't call me Lynx, call me Bob.	**Bobcat**

Did you know?

The Bobcat is common to the Ozark and throughout North America. It is the smallest cat in the Lynx family and is a fierce, solitary hunter with a mild dislike for Shakespeare and all things Lynx. So call him Bob.

Nuts & Bolts-This is a poem written for two voices that can be read out loud in a back and forth manner as individuals or in two groups.

The Butcher Bird

A songbird singing understated,
its fierceness very underrated.

When impaling hapless prey,
its demeanor gets meaner I'd say.

You won't mistake it for a Robin
When you see it shish-kaboboin.

Never picky, that's what I've heard,
so don't offend the Butcher Bird.

Did you know?

The Loggerhead Shrike (Butcher Bird) proves that first impressions count but aren't always entirely true. A Shrike is a lovely Ozark songbird that impales its food (insects and rodents) on a natural fork like a thorn or sharp branch before eating. Shish kabob anyone?

Nuts & Bolts-This poem is made up of groups of two lines called "couplets." Couplets don't have to rhyme but often do.

Doin' Business

Coyotes, they are known to sell
their urine and some do quite well.
Apparently this oddity
to some is a commodity.

I find this strange and so surprising,
in spite of being enterprising
some coyote entrepreneur
couldn't peddle their manure.

Did you know?

Coyote urine (or pee) is used as a repellant in gardens to keep away animals such as deer, rabbits, and opossums. It is available at your local yard care shop as well as wholesale from enterprising Ozark coyotes.

Nuts & Bolts-A stanza is a group of poetic lines that are often repeated according to a fixed pattern. This poem contains four-line stanzas called "quatrains."

The Evil Chicken

Amongst the foxes, mice, and owls
and the mounds of deer manure--
there dwells a prairie chicken,
who is haunted-that's for sure.

Its eyes are red, its beak coal black
and its feathers are disheveled—
but the strangest thing I ever saw…
the eggs it laid were deviled.

Did you know?

The Prairie Chicken has become almost extinct, it
once thrived in the Ozark where grassland and
woodland converged. Although the hens can lay
between 5 and 17 eggs per clutch, none of them are
deviled.

Nuts & Bolts-Punctuation can be used effectively in
a poem and works well when you need that slight
pause to set up the next line for emphasis.

Battle of Wits
(A poem for two voices)

Seize the lure in its allure,   **Fisherman**
Squeeze with all your might.
Wheeze my feisty trophy fish.
Freeze you on ice tonight.

Vicious sport, I must retort,   **Trout**
Malicious game you spin it.
Fictitious is your storyline.
Judicious fish will win it!

Please don't pout my elite trout,   **Fisherman**
These falsehoods are no virtue.
Tease with bait till you give up.
Appease us or "we'll hurt you."

Fishes revel in your misses,   **Trout**
Suspicious of your tempting bait.
Militias (soldier fishes) are we.
Ambitious odds of one in eight.

Did you know?

Rainbow trout are the most common trout in the Ozark.
Some are gullible and easily caught but there are plenty of
well educated specimens that require a good deal of luck
and tempting bait to bring to net.

Nuts & Bolts-This poem contains "front rhyme" where the
rhyming words are at the beginning of each line. Notice I use
a consistent rhyme for each voice.

Ted

Ted the cannibalistic tick
is not so good at arithmetic.

He eats those ticks, yes quite a few,
then loses count before he's through.

It's so uncouth to eat your kind,
but don't tell Ted, he doesn't mind.

Dear Ted, my pleading don't ignore,
it's fine to be a carnivore
but this advice it should suffice,
learn to count and switch to lice.

Did you know?

Ticks can get so plentiful in certain parts of the
Ozark that they have been known to kill a deer.
They thrive in thick Bermuda grass and will feast on
each other if they can't find a natural host, so Ted,
watch out!

Nuts & Bolts-Line arrangement is important in this
poem, notice I start with rhyming couplets and end
with the four line, quatrain. This sets apart the
pleading and advice part of the poem.

Gray Matter

Some shrews will plant geraniums
to calm their stressed out craniums.

It keeps their brains so brilliant,
enormous yet resilient.

Other shrews choose playing chess
to help relieve the awful stress

that comes with such a cerebellum
so dense pet shops refuse to sell 'em.

Did you know?

The Northern Short-Tailed Shrew is common to the Ozark and holds nearly 10% of its body mass in its brain. That is the highest brain to body mass ratio of all animals. Pet shops won't sell shrews because of the additional expense of chess sets and garden tools.

Nuts & Bolts-This poem contains full or exact rhyme where the words begin differently but the vowels and all sounds that follow match such as with "chess" and "stress."

Last Respects

I found myself caught quite off guard
not versed in funeral etiquette.
Folks traveled from as far away
as Utah and Connecticut.

The mourners stood in disbelief,
my shock I couldn't mask it.
The corpse-we watched it move a bit
then climb right out the casket.

At first I thought it morbid
but really it's quite awesome.
I hear he does this now and then
and calls it "playin' possum."

Did you know?

The opossum, North America's only marsupial, will
play dead for hours if necessary when threatened
by a predator. If you are invited to an Ozark
'possum's funeral just send flowers because that
trickster is likely alive and well.

Nuts & Bolts-Humor and the element of surprise
are important in this poem. Always try to have your
poem be grounded in reality for best effect.

Onion Thief

Sam sneaks into gardens
in the quiet of the night
to steal those tasty onions
but stealing is not right.

He took ten yellow onions
from a garden just last week.
Then snuck back in on Tuesday
but only took a leek.

Did you know?

Onions provide a tasty treat to animals in the Ozark.
Black bears will eat them by the hundreds and have
been known to "borrow" from backyard gardens.
When Sam takes a "leek" without asking he is
stealing a more refined, subtle member of the onion
family.

Nuts & Bolts-This is an example of wordplay where
humor and wit are used to amuse the reader with
double and ambiguous word meanings such as with
the word "leek."

Yeti's Promise

Yeti made a privy promise
between him and Sheriff Thomas.
Pledgin' to stay out of trouble
in lieu of costs with fines double.
One night, the Yeti, out from hidin,'
tryin' to be law abidin,'
had the urge to "kick it."

Root beer lead to sassafrassin'
so he was cited for harassin'
bystanders and pedestrians.
Then we mad equestrians,
gathered sticks and tawny ropes.
Some read their horoscopes in hopes
of guidance in the thicket.

The search, it lingered on for days
then somethin' moved beyond the haze.
It spooked the horses and the men.
We heard it once and then again.
In that darkness he approached us,
then smiled and said "Buenos noches,
how 'bout a game of cricket?"

Not lookin' for a fight that night
we played cricket by the moonlight.
The game, was too complex for us
and he played ambidextrous
but we kept on appeasin' him
and no one teased him on a whim,
yet he began to picket.

"Your promise, Yeti, that's why we're here
just pay your fine, no need to fear,"
"We've searched and you've eluded us."
"Don't picket and be rude to us."
Then Yeti ran, the chase was on.
We almost caught him but he's gone…
and someone paid the ticket.

Did you know?

A large section of Missouri is Ozark territory with 85 reported Yeti (Big Foot) sightings to date. The Yeti has been known to sip chamomile tea with a cat-like creature called the Ozark Holler after a good game of cricket.

Nuts & Bolts-This narrative poem has character, voice, plot and conflict much like those used in other forms of writing only with fewer words in general.

Ken Slesarik

**Fast-food Chain
(Over 30 Billion Served)**

The morning crowd of hungry flies
means our menu's no surprise.
We serve one thing no matter---
it's the breakfast poo-poo platter.

We offer meals for other species,
such as toads who dislike feces.
They choose to hop and stop for lunch
to eat those flies up by the bunch.

The toads then do a double take
and learn they're dinner for the snake.
Still some partake in snake, like owls.
Our drive-thru is for hungry fowls.

Did you know?

Fast-food chains are all over the Ozark and cater to
busy on-the-go critters such as flies, toads, snakes
and fowls. In actuality, a food chain illustrates how
living things get their food and most animals are
part of several food chains that in turn form a food
web.

Nuts & Bolts-This poem uses "internal rhyme"
where rhyming words are placed in the middle of
lines and not just on the ends. The words "hop" and
"stop" are one example. Can you find the other?

Ozark Hellbender
(Eastern Salamander)

Hellbenders, hellbenders,
those youthful offenders,
yes I believe they conspire.

Hellbenders, hellbenders,
refusing suspenders
or belts to wear for attire.

Hellbenders, hellbenders,
from both bender genders
in trendsetting they never tire.

Hellbenders, hellbenders,
new fads you invent,
hellbenders, hellbenders:
Hell-bent!

Did you know?

The Ozark Hellbender is a unique aquatic
salamander that can reach lengths of nearly two
feet. They live in the clean, clear rivers of the Ozark
and have fleshy folds of baggy skin to go with their
baggy, trend-setting, belt-less pants.

Nuts & Bolts-This poem uses repetition like the
refrain in a song to give it a musical quality.

A Lady Cusses

When a ladybug starts to cuss
I find it so ridiculous.
It's also wrong and very shocking;
one cussed at me while I was walking.

She followed me and got real loud
with words that'd make a sailor proud.
So I yelled back unceasingly
until a bumble bee stung me.

The lesson learned, don't shout or talk
to Ozark insects on your walk
and resist the urge, ignore the tug,
when cussed out by a ladybug.

Did you know?

The Asian Lady Beetle has been introduced to the Ozark to help naturally control pest populations that were damaging crops. Although very similar to the native species, this Lady Beetle can be a little feisty in action and speech.

Nuts & Bolts-Using basic common words to rhyme such as "talk" and "walk" can make unique rhyme and variations such as "unceasingly" and "bee stung me" stand out.

Contagious Charlie

While waiting for his appendectomy
he had the gall to sit right next to me.

I sure wish he hadn't sat beside us
because now we have appendicitis.

Did you know?

According to a Duke University study, animals such as the opossum and rabbit have an appendix much like humans. Appendicitis is not contagious but if it were I'm sure, Ozark critters would comfort each other throughout their respective surgeries.

Nuts & Bolts-This poem has a creative use of rhyme. Usually it is better to place the more complex word second such as in the second couplet but I also choose to switch it in the first couplet by placing the unique word first.

The Roadkill Café

At the famous Roadkill Café
they serve a delightful buffet,
coyotes, toads, squirrels and rabbits
have really changed my eating habits.
When carcass taste was new to me
I never left gratuity
but now I just can't tip enough
for that fleshy, freshly flattened stuff.
Scraped from the highway or avenue.
I'm sure you've tried it, haven't you?

Did you know?

When all the data are combined, some
researchers now suggest that animals who perish
on the road may exceed the total number of all
other causes. This might explain why Ozark
'possum pie is plentiful.

Nuts & Bolts-Except for "rabbits" and "habits" all of
the rhymes in this poem contain visual variations.

Dapper Dan

Meet Dapper Dan the "ladies' man."
Now I'm not a fan of Dapper Dan.
It's the hair from his face and nose
that's in need of a trim and it shows.

He thinks it's cool. I think it's gross
that a mustache grows from his nose.
He just ignores it, yet there it lies,
underneath five beady eyes.

Did you know?

All Robber Flies have stout, spiny legs and a dense
mustache of bristles on the face with 3 simple eyes
between two large compound eyes. I'm sure a
bristly face and five eyes are very attractive to other
Ozark Robber Flies.

Nuts & Bolts-The end words "gross" and "nose" are
slant or near rhymes with a slight difference in
sound.

Big-Eared Bat

He's a little fella, short,
with soft, gigantic ears
and he sings a cappella,
bringing ladies to tears.

No sooner does the crooner
start to sing his song
when a lady in the crowd
begins to hum along.

Next it gets complex
but it soon becomes apparent
the little big-eared crooner
will soon become a parent.

Did you know?

The Ozark Big-Eared bat is aptly named for its over-sized ears. Mating among these bats is initiated with ritualized calls and singing. They pass their velvety voice onto their offspring as a single pup is born in May or June.

Red Tailed Hawk
(Chicken Hawk)

As a mood booster

we introduced her

to the rooster-

this amused her.

Did you know?

The Red-Tailed Hawk is one of three species collectively known in the United States as the "chicken hawk" though it rarely preys on chickens. Ozark chicken hawks are big advocates of the celebrity-chicken free diet. Go figure.

Tumbling Class

When gazing through
my looking glass
I saw what seemed
a tumbling class
of ten cartwheeling
cat-like varmints,
dressed in spandex
work-out garments.
As I got close,
I smelled this funk
and sure enough,
a startled skunk
cartwheeled away
to tell the others
but then that band
of furry brothers
asked with such a
happy zeal
if I'd like to learn
to cartwheel?
It's good for some
but why the fuss?
It's dangerous
for most of us.
Furthermore,
I couldn't stay
'cuz I can't stand
their funky spray.

Did you know?

The presence of a Striped Skunk in the Ozark is sometimes first apparent by its odor. It can emit a highly unpleasant odor when it feels threatened and will often do a cartwheel while spraying to warn other skunks of danger. Wear spandex and bring a clothes pin for your nose if you take their class.

#1 Allergy Symptom

Allergies bring itchy eyes.
If one gets hives, it's no surprise.
But number one, I forgot.
Is it coughs? No, it's snot.

Did you know?

Ozark animals such as the bobcat can suffer from inhalant allergies to pollen. Inhalant allergies can result in asthmatic symptoms, as well as itching. Never offer a wild animal a tissue, no matter how uncomfortable they may look.

Psychic on the Run

Marge the Ozark groundhog,
whose predictions seldom fail,
she has a guarded secret,
she escaped from county jail.

Measuring ten inches,
with a crystal ball that's Marge.
So be on the lookout for
a small medium at large.

Did you know?

The old belief regarding Groundhog Day is widely
accepted in the Ozark. Marge emerges from her
burrow on February 2nd to see if it's sunny. If she
sees her shadow it means she's "predicting" winter
will continue for six more weeks. Lately she's been
lyin' low.

Nuts & Bolts-Rhyme scheme is a way of
representing the pattern of rhyme in a poem or
stanza. This poem has an a, b, c, b rhyme scheme
in its stanzas as the second and fourth lines rhyme.

Safe Haven

Ozark snails will undergo
lugging their shells like cargo.
Most choose not to venture out,
for one reason I've no doubt-
they fear becoming escargot.

Did you know?

Escargot (pronounced es-car-go) is a dish of
cooked land snails, usually served as an appetizer.
Typically the snails are removed from their shells,
gutted, cooked, and then poured back into their
shells, the stuff of nightmares for these Ozark
mollusks.

Nuts & Bolts-This poem is a limerick. A limerick is
a humorous verse made up of five lines with an a, a,
b, b, a rhyme scheme.

Insect Epithets

Here lies the lowly Doodle Bug
with his talent to create.
He spent his days in solitude
sketching invertebrates.

Here lies eclectic centipede
with her clothes in hues of blues.
She spent her days in thrift shops
in search of funky shoes.

Here lies the Dog Faced Butterfly
who was kind and lived to please.
He spent his daytime barking
and his nights just scratching fleas.

Did you know?

Insects have a shorter lifespan in comparison to
other Ozark wildlife such as bears and foxes. The
doodle bug, centipede, and dog-faced butterfly lie in
unmarked graves at the Ozark cemetery for bugs.

Nuts & Bolts-Enjambment is when a line of a poem
runs over to the next line without a natural pause or
punctuation such as in every two lines in this poem.

Ozark Summer Haiku
(rhyming version)

Summer's just scorchin'.
record highs and misfortune,
non-flammable fur.

Ozark Summer Haiku
(traditional version)

Summer is scorching
fans, hats, sunglasses and sweat,
non-flammable fur.

Did you know?

In the Arkansas Ozark, the warmest month of the year is July. The highest temperature recorded in Arkansas is 120, Fahrenheit on August 10, 1936 at Ozark. Non-flammable fur has been the rage ever since.

Nuts & Bolts-A haiku is a three-line Japanese form that generally focuses on nature. The first and third lines have five syllables and the second has seven.

Glass Lizard

It was to be a brouhaha
but "ha", it surely wasn't.
Some said it must have really hurt
but no sir, well it doesn't.

My brittle tail, it broke like glass
but I give you this assurance,
soon I'll be as good as new
for I purchased glass insurance.

Did you know?

The Glass Lizard is often mistaken for a snake,
however, it has external ear holes and is in the
lizard family. It's brittle tail will often break off and
continue to move to distract predators so they can
escape deep into the Ozark.

Skin Deep

"Beauty is only skin deep,"
she said with a boastful grin.

But I can't bear to tell her,
the skin she's in is quite thin.

Did you know?

The Turkey Vulture, with its bald, red head, is found throughout the Ozark. While eating the carcass of dead animals its head serves an important function, as it does not pick up unwanted pieces of meat and bacteria. That would be unbecoming when gazing into the mirror.

Nuts & Bolts-When performing poetry sometimes it is better to start with a short, easy to read poem. Remember things like volume, fluency, pronunciation, and expression.

Forty Winks
(Eastern Gray Squirrel)

Never an insomniac,
they clearly have a natural knack
for deep rest and relaxation.
Just don't call it hibernation.

If only we could sleep like these,
for fifteen hours catching z's.
It's the pleasure I'd pursue
to soundly sleep, wouldn't you?

I'd pitch that slumber formula
to retirees down in Florida.
Dreaming dreams with a peaceful theme,
I'd charge for this per diem.

Did you know?

Gray Squirrels are found in wooded areas
throughout the Ozark. They can sleep up to 15
hours a day but do not hibernate. When awake they
often travel along power lines, sometimes shorting
out transformers or entire substations, helping
people catch their z's.

Nuts & Bolts-This poem has an a, a, b, b rhyme
scheme in its stanzas as the first two lines rhyme
and the third and fourth lines have a different
rhyme.

Small Talk

He chirps and thinks that he endears
but only sings and never hears.
On and on he blabs, it's endless,
you'd think that it would leave him friendless.

Alone with others, there he dwells,
with those who like to hear themselves.

Did you know?

During the breeding season in the Ozark, some
birds sing practically non-stop. The Red-eyed Vireo
(Vireo olivaceus) has been recorded singing 'see
me-hear me' 22,197 times in one day. That's a lot of
"small talk."

Timely Advice

Toby's tattered Timex
told terrible time,
so why he sold his Seiko
I'll never know.

But I won't soon forget
his timely advice,
for he turned to me and said
"Wait a minute."

Did you know?

Some animals instinctively sense when to migrate or spawn but others such as the Eastern Chipmunk do not seem to consciously determine specific lengths of time. That's why a newer, reliable watch is important for Ozark animals such as Toby.

Nuts & Bolts-This poem uses alliteration which is the repetition of consonants, especially as the initial sound in a string of words (**T**oby's **t**attered **T**imex **t**old **t**errible **t**ime…).

The Woodland Vole

The Woodland Vole
prefers to stroll,
walking leisurely.

A tiny soul,
the Woodland Vole,
don't chase it, let it be.

The Woodland Vole
just doesn't know,
when fleeing fast and free,

how very slow,
the Woodland Vole
can seem to you and me.

Did you know?

Woodland Voles genuinely like to live and move
underground but have been timed running above
ground at speeds reaching three point eight miles
per hour for 25 feet. Woodland Voles will often enter
Ozark sprint competitions and do very well against
snails and turtles.

Nuts & Bolts-This poem has 3 line stanzas called
"triplets." Notice how the words "The Woodland
Vole" alternate placement in the stanzas to give it a
rhythmic quality.

Swan Song

If you should ever walk up on
a trumpeteering swan,
carry on, carry on
leave that trumpeteering fellow.

If you should ever walk up on
a cello playing swan,
ask the swan, ask the swan
for a solo on the cello.

It's really rather moving.

Did you know?

The Trumpeter Swan has a deep, loud trumpet-like
call. This snow-white creature is the largest native
waterfowl species in North America and has a
wingspan of more than 7 feet with a height of about
4 feet. Perfect for playing the trumpet or cello for
adoring Ozark fans.

Nuts & Bolts-This poem has a consistent pattern of
beats or stresses that convey a sense of rhythm or
movement.

32 Bonus Poems

My Distressed Poem

Can you fix this poem?
Dr. Seuss I'm surely not.
It's not a sonnet or an ode
with a complicated plot.
It's closer to a limerick,
a basic, simple jaunt.
The best parts of my poem
are the paper and the font.
The meter it is woeful,
the cadence clearly weak.
My grammar needs some work
so go on and take a peek.
Please do your best to fix this.
I'm certain you won't fail.
And if you know a publisher,
this poem, it's for sale.

Odd Verse

If you're not adverse to odd verse

then my verse is no worse

and I dare not say superior,

'cause my rhymes are known to cause a rash

on many a posterior.

Where's the Undertaker?

When death came calling and souls took flight,
'twas much to the undertakers delight,
society's dregs, a hideous lot
and ghoulish caretakers of graveyard plots.

As the years rolled by, by sheer attrition,
they became known as mere morticians.
You'll find them now in private sectors,
listed under "Funeral Directors."

Commander Thomas

I, Lieutenant Cornwall Thomas,
battle tested, make this promise;

although tantamount to treason
goin' commando's out of season,

so I'll wear my thermal underwear,
concealing ample derriere

from botched cosmetic surgery
and Botox on the buttocks.

Ou' Sont les Toilettes?
(Where's the Toilet?)

John Harrington invented the first flushing toilet.
Engineers took years to perfect and not spoil it.

Joseph Bramah improved on the old water closet
with parts that connected like one big composite.

Thomas Crapper, improvement, he surely pursued it.
His toilet, they laughed, they snickered and booed it.

But after awhile they poo pooed it.

Ms. Cratchit's Contraction Comments
(School for Wayward Children 1910)

Please use them very sparingly.
These little words lack virtue.
Apostrophes can be your friend,
Appease them, they won't hurt you.

Ambitious overuse my son,
Repetitious, a distraction.
Vicious is my grading, child,
Malicious, the contraction. (D-)

Root Veggies

I despise that shameful swagga
of an unclothed rutabaga

and radishes are very rude,
especially when in the nude.

Those prancing parsnips never clothed,
that's one sight I've always loathed.

I'd like to coldly cast a curse
on unbecoming beets and worse

those turnips lacking underwear,
it pains me so but I just stare.

Lastly, lowly burdock roots
are clad in nothing and in cahoots.

It's all wrong and so distressing.
I prefer them in ranch dressing.

Cowboy Woes

City slicker, shyster, hipster!
Shoulda roped that low-down tipster.
He said, "The zebra is a force."
"Don't put your money on the horse."
Then stole my gal and kissed her.

Drawing Conclusions

I am an artist,
both fun and free,
but painting and acrylics
are not for me.

While others like sculpture,
canvas and crafts,
I draw conclusions
with revisions and drafts.

I don't need an easel,
paper or pen.
Yet I draw and create
for hours on end.

If you think I'm crazy,
and suffer delusion,
well you've just drawn
your own conclusion.

Wendell's Dilemma

Wendell Winston Whooping Crane
dreams of riding atop a train
to west Zargoza but can't decide
which train car he would like to ride.
Is it the engine or caboose?
He seems to try but just can't choose.
Each day again there's not much gain.
He just can't choose betwixt the twain.

Reckless Driver

He liked to polish his Polish automobile,
then recklessly drive behind the wheel.
No license or permit to permit him to drive;
no signal or seatbelt to keep him alive.

He'd eat fried bass and play bass guitar,
at the same time driving his red sports car.
His foot it was lead, likes to be in the lead,
he got 43 tickets for dangerous speed.

He refused an order, called an officer refuse,
then cursed the officer's nieces and nephews.
Although he's a rebel and likes to rebel,
he now spends his days in a five by ten cell.

Holding a Conversation

It's delightful to converse with you
and grasp just what you say.
When I try holding a conversation,
it just gets away.
The words I hold unmercifully,
they always seem to slip.
Help me hold this conversation please.
I'm sure it's just my grip.

My Stylist

Shampoo, condition, crimp or braid,
when Momma helps I'm not afraid.
She'll wash and comb then style my hair
as I sit in my rocking chair.

I should wear ribbons, ribbons and bows.
Should I wear ribbons, ribbons and bows?

I'm not afraid 'cause Momma knows.

The Peculiar Mosquito

Something landed on my arm
with a sweet and simple grace,
a mosquito with a curlicue
cascading down her face.

There was no mistaking it
for she seemed to be raking it
or combing it, that curlicue
cascading down her face.

The curlicue, it blocked her view
so I squashed her flat,
the mosquito with a curlicue
cascading down her face.

The Chef's Surprise

His Majesty was wroth at the palace chef,
who dare serve broth and pudding of porpoise.

He threw kingly fits and porpoise pudding,
of course, it's not befitting a king.

In mournful costume the shell of a chef
sits in the anteroom playing Parcheesi.

This prelim to the brouhaha tickles me
as the dimwit cook awaits his fate.

He starts to perspire so I drink tea
with Devonshire cream to lighten the mood.

At long last the king speaks his decree
in a whisper from centuries past.

"Your head on this plate, wicked servant".
Wait, he's talking to me? The royal taster!

Job Description

Pathologists can be demented,
their work immortalized, cemented.
With job description oft' unclear-
such is a sidewalk engineer.

Cardiologists are complex chaps,
never ones for dice or craps.
They count the cards and count the cost
and play until their money's lost.

The Watchsmith

As an expert watchsmith

he'll surly fix your watch with

the utmost dexterity,

a smile and a guarantee.

Trust Sasquatch with your watch.

His work is really top notch.

So for top-notch watch repair

bring it in if you dare.

My Problem

I eat those healthy vegetables,
greens of every kind.

They keep me fit and strong
in my body and my mind.

With broccoli for breakfast
and collard greens for lunch;

green peas by the handful,
and lettuce by the bunch.

You'd think with all this greenery,
my life, it would be great,

a healthy glow with energy,
at an ideal weight.

It seems I found a side effect,
to say that would be fair.

I've got sprouts of leafy spinach,
instead of curly hair.

The doctor says that I should add
more protein to my diet.

What's to lose? Look at me.
Perhaps I need to try it.

That's Unappealing

I find it appalling yet strangely appealing
when some people slip their body goes reeling.

I try not to laugh but just get a feeling,
seeing them fall on a peel or a peeling.

When I slip on a peeling it's not so appealing.
I flip through the air, my body goes reeling.

When they laugh at me, I just get a feeling,
laughing at others is so unappealing.

Chasing Excellence

Chasing excellence
with full focus
is the focus
of my endeavor.

Winning the gold
is a must.
A lifeline I must
never sever.

For to be a winner
I fully focus,
that I must.........
and win however.

An Inside Tip

I wager money just because
that's what a racetrack bookie does.
An insiders' tip that I propose,
the zebra wins it by a nose.
So don't waste money and resources.
It's my job to know the racehorses.
When the zebra wins and not a horse
you'll split the cash with me of course.

Cindy Chantilla

Cindy Marie Chantilla,
the viola-playing chinchilla,
begins with a confident grin
when she puts viola to chin.

Her music she knows it by rote
and she rarely plays a bad note.

But oh when she does
it's likely because

some sneaky baboon or gorilla,
drank Cindy's sarsaparilla.

Itchy Dilemma

Our dilemma was daunting
resembling a haunting
with twitching and itching –
positively bewitching.

We were itching our itches
on our backs and our britches,
shedding clothes (every stich)
yet continued to itch.

So we'd run in mad dashes,
scratching patches of rashes,
all the while we were cloaked
in poisonous oak!

Nightfall

I grapple with the question
when each night I close my eyes.
Why do we call it nightfall,
could it not be called nightrise?

What's even more perplexing
are my thoughts when I awake,
because at sundown night falls…
then day breaks.

Big Foot

If you see the reclusive Yeti
it's unwise to serve him spaghetti.
He's also known as Sasquatch
and if he's been playing hopscotch
his stomach is likely churning
and spaghetti leaves it burning.
So if you serve it, I really feel
it'd be wise to offer chamomile.

Gargoyles

Gargoyle, Gargoyle

in your typical way

you never take time

for Gargoyolous play.

Gargoyle, Gargoyle

you spend your days toiling

doing what Gargoyles do…

Gargoyling.

Elephant Advice

Don't take offense
to odd elefense
and please never hunt
the proud elefunt
but do take a stance
with those elefance
who wear striped pants
litered with lint-
the elefint.

River Sippin'

Simply sippin' from the Mississippi,
sadly never seemed to simply satisfy me.

So I sipped some samples from the Nile,
but grew tired of sippin' after awhile.

Then I sipped some lakes, but I digress,
'cause the best sippin' place is the Tigress.

The Tendrils are Coming

If you're haunted by a tendril
it's so tempting to ignore,
creeping ever steaith-fully,
advancing towards your door.

A tendril may seem dignified,
like a Duke or Duchess,
until that tendril has you
in its greedy grasp and clutches.

A tapestry of tendril
on the lattice I deplore,
for once those tendrils have you,
you'll be gone forevermore.

Dad's Keys

We searched high, low,
over, below,
backwards, up down
and all around.
Then what a wonder,
just right under
leftover peas,
dad found his keys.

Halitosis

A whiff of breath,
impossible
to partake of.

Rotten, reeking,
vile and vengeful.
Hints of Cheetos.

The sad saga,
to tell or not?
I think not.

For now
I'll be polite,
feigning
puppy breath.

Money Talks?

Does money talk? I just don't know.
My allowance seems to say "hello."
But if it talks, I just can't tell,
except the times it says "farewell."

ABOUT THE AUTHOR

I am a teacher and poet from Phoenix, Arizona and the proud father to Kenny, Cathy and Bonnie.

It is my mission to transform students by getting them to believe in themselves through the medium of poetry and my "Heroes and Poets" assembly program has been well received by administrators, teachers, parents and children.

CREATURES, CRITTERS, BEASTS and VARMINTS is my lively poetry collection that combines fun and science as I examine both familiar and unique wildlife. CCBV contains 32 wildlife poems along with 31 unique facts. I also include 32 bonus poems and 25 poetry tips to encourage children to write their own verse.

In addition I am part of the Poetry Friday Anthology series along with many of today's most prolific authors. "The Woodland Vole" and a version of "Small Talk" originally appeared in THE POETRY FRIDAY ANTHOLOGY K-5 EDITION.

To contact me with questions or to check my availability for school visits or conferences please visit kenslesarik.com.

Heroes and Poets

"Heroes and Poets" is my assembly program that grew out of my motivation to help children become their best and my love of poetry.

My goal when I visit a school is to have a lasting impact that goes beyond one afternoon and I stand ready to serve.

For more information and to check my availability please visit kenslesarik.com and click the "Contact Me" tab.

Ken Slesarik

Poetry begins in delight and ends in wisdom.

Robert Frost

Ken Slesarik

www.ingramcontent.com/pod-product-compliance
Lightning Source LLC
Chambersburg PA
CBHW060201070426
42447CB00033B/2258